The Invisible Children

nipping failure in the bud

Virginia Makins

(with photographs by Paul Allen)

edited by

Patricia Kendell

David Fulton Publishers

London

David Fulton Publishers Ltd
2 Barbon Close, London WC1N 3JX

First published in Great Britain by David Fulton Publishers 1997

Note: The right of Virginia Makins to be identified as the author of this work has been asserted by her in accordance with the Copyright, Designs and Patents Act 1988.

Copyright © The National Pyramid Trust
Cover photographs © Christopher Jones and Paul Allen

British Library Cataloguing in Publication Data

A catalogue record for this book is available from the British Library

ISBN 1–85346–492–9

Typeset by The Harrington Consultancy Ltd.
Printed in Great Britain by Bell & Bain Ltd., Glasgow

Contents

Foreword

The Gulbenkian Foundation first learnt about the method of work developed and espoused by the National Pyramid Trust, described in these pages, some three years ago when the Trust's founder and director, Kay FitzHerbert, approached us about the possibility of financial support. That method – the screening of children of primary school age and the opportunity for the particularly vulnerable among them to join special after-school clubs and have their self-esteem and confidence gradually built up – appeared to have three distinctive characteristics. First, it was concerned with children whose needs might not be conspicuously problematic, the 'invisible children' of the book's title, but who nonetheless required special attention if their problems were not to accompany them through to secondary education and beyond. Second, the method was strikingly simple: it was based on a straightforward, uncomplicated set of principles which had proved to be effective. Finally, and related to this, it was clearly replicable: there was no reason why it should not be adopted by others elsewhere. And it was because the Foundation believed that such a development would be both beneficial and timely that we offered funds for the commissioning of this publication. We hope the availability of Virginia Makins' succinct account of the method will encourage schools and local authorities with little or no knowledge of it to reflect on its potential value and consider its adoption. The publication appears at a propitious moment for the National Pyramid Trust as it begins to promote its work nationwide. We hope that it will help that process and, in so doing, play its part in drawing to the attention of schools and others the needs of children who might otherwise remain invisible.

Simon Richey
Assistant Director (Education)
Calouste Gulbenkian Foundation (UK Branch)
October 1996

---

*I became a founder Trustee for its first two years, resigning to research this report.

Preface

This is the story of the National Pyramid Trust (NPT): how it started, how it operates, and its prospects for the future. My own interest started when I was working for the *Times Educational Supplement* in 1989, and wrote an article about the scheme[1], then running in the London Borough of Hounslow.

The Trust was set up in 1992 to build on the successful Hounslow experience and to explore ways of extending the project nationally.* The Trust secured funding from the Department of Health and the Norman Trust for pilot projects in two new areas, in order to trial materials and procedures in readiness for taking the scheme still further afield.

It became clear that it would be helpful to have an account of the story so far, describing the origins and theoretical basis of the work: how it was evolving in the pilot areas; the results; and the Trust's plans for future expansion.

In order to help make the scheme more widely known the Gulbenkian Foundation generously provided the funds for this report. The fieldwork was done in the summer of 1995, when the pilot projects were in their second year.

I would like to thank several people who have made this report possible: Simon Richey of the Gulbenkian Foundation first suggested that such a report would be useful; the staff of the National Pyramid Trust were endlessly patient and helpful – the administrator, Audrey Harrison, responded uncomplainingly to a stream of requests for documents and information; and Eleanor Armitage and Patricia Morris, the co-ordinators of the pilot projects in Bristol and Hillingdon, gave me a great deal of time and introduced me to the schools.

The heads, teachers and volunteer club-leaders in the four schools I visited could not have been more hospitable, allowing me to sit in on sensitive meetings and take part in sessions of Pyramid Clubs. They gave me valuable feedback and put me in touch with some parents to find out their views of the scheme. The only condition was that all schools and children remained anonymous. All names have been changed in the text. I apologise if a name of someone once involved in a Pyramid club has been used – the name does not refer to that actual person.

Patricia Kendell was an ideal editor, sensitive to the style and intentions of both author and the National Pyramid Trust.

Finally, this report, like the whole project, would not have happened without the inspiration and determination of Kay FitzHerbert, Founder and Director of the National Pyramid Trust.

Virginia Makins
London
October 1996

v

INTRODUCTION

The Invisible Children

Lucy never sees her own mother and her step-mother is jealous and rejects her; she is bright but making no progress at school and has no friends.

Winston is a loveable child, but so very quiet. Asthmatic and possibly over-protected – he has no friends and plays on his own.

Chirrag is small for his age with a rather odd appearance and a speech problem which means he can't articulate properly. Many difficulties at home. He has friends but is underachieving at school.

Fatima is a loner at school, very withdrawn and does not relate to other children.

Mark is immature, clinging to adults. He irritates the other children and is disliked and bullied by them.

Figure 1 Having fun and gaining self-confidence

Children who have either significantly greater difficulties in learning than their peers, a disability which hinders their normal progress or severe behaviour problems, are generally picked up under the Special Education Needs Code of Practice. But children like Lucy, Winston, Chirrag, Fatima and Mark, whose needs are less obvious, can be overlooked. In a busy classroom, they are often invisible.

Such children do not require special educational provision as defined by the Code of Practice but their inability to relate to others or their social isolation and unhappiness gives teachers cause for concern. Their problems usually arise from some sort of stress in their lives which damages their self-esteem and potential to achieve. Lucy, for example, lives with her father in a chaotic reconstituted family of six where she is the only girl.

Unless preventive action is taken quickly, there is a real danger that these vulnerable children will flounder in secondary schools. Their primary teachers may well have spotted warning signs, but without intervention of some kind, many children will end up as educational and social failures, with all the costs to themselves, and to the health and social services, that this entails.

The National Pyramid Trust was founded to promote a low-cost, practical scheme to help all such children: 7- or 8-year-old children, who have developed a sense of failure, are still young enough to be open to change. A boost to their self-confidence at this stage can have dramatic and lasting effects.

CHAPTER 1

Starting Points

Many good practical innovations start with one person. In the 1970s, Kay FitzHerbert was the social worker on an Educational Priority Area (EPA) project attached to a high school and its feeder primaries in the London Borough of Ealing. At the time, many social workers had a stereotype of teachers as uncaring and uninterested in children's social, family and emotional problems. Kay found that they cared deeply, but because they felt powerless and frustrated they often repressed their concerns. She became aware of what she calls 'the lunacy' of primary teachers seeing clear danger signals of future failure for individual children, but having no available system of early intervention or strategies to prevent it.

The Need for Early Intervention

Existing support systems did not seem to be capable of *preventive* action. Indeed, although social workers, educational psychologists or health workers often said, when children hit the buffers at secondary school, 'If only we'd seen this child earlier', in practice prevention was not really on the agenda.

Kay found that there was no accepted practice about whether and when to turn to support services to address the needs of such children. Everything depended on the widely differing views and practices of head teachers. Left to themselves, class teachers did not have time, or proven strategies, to help children whose problems were social, emotional or physical in origin rather than academic. The first priority for educational psychologists was children with severe learning and behaviour problems; social workers only contacted schools when there was a possibility of care proceedings.

She became convinced that early intervention must at least be tried. Prevention *had* to be cheaper than remedial effort later and was more likely to improve the well-being and future prospects of the children concerned. As a social worker, she wanted to see proper casework begin much earlier for such children.

Finding a Model that Works

One possible model was the routine screening used by the School Health Service. Originally every child was briefly screened at least twice in its primary career. Then doctors decided their time would be better spent giving the neediest children 20 minutes each, rather than spending four minutes on each child.

So a system developed where teachers and doctors sat down together and went through a whole class list, comparing past notes and knowledge about every child. The doctor then saw only the children causing concern. Kay decided that a routine screening system which covered children's social and emotional development as well as their physical health would be the ideal basis for promoting prevention.

In 1978 the Social Science Research Council (SSRC) gave her a three-year grant to develop 'an integrated, preventive childcare system focused on the primary school'. The London Borough of Hounslow took on the action research project and three of its primary schools agreed to try out a scheme to screen all children and to involve other professionals in helping those showing early signs of difficulties.

It was a good time to try to get such interdisciplinary meetings going: the report of the enquiry into the case of Maria Colwell, who died due to the failure of education, health and social services to communicate at grass-roots level, was still fresh in people's minds.

In many ways the meetings that first year went well. Teachers voiced their concerns and other agencies offered information and ideas about how to intervene and help. Teachers valued the advice and new strategies. But when it came to asking for practical action, there tended to be a deathly hush. The early intervention and casework did not happen. When challenged about this, one health visitor summed up the problem:

> 'If nobody has committed a crime or cried for help, I can't wade in and tell a mother how to bring up her kids.'

Therapeutic Activity Groups

Kay cast around for another way to intervene with at least some children. An Australian social worker suggested starting a club for them. Kay had no experience of group work, and little hope that it could have any significant impact. But her project had two years to run, the schools had been promised some action to help children they had identified, and something had to be done. Without enthusiasm, she agreed to try the club idea.

An after-school club was planned, to run for ten sessions. A social worker who was also a nun led it, helped by a social work student on a work placement. The children chose their club's name – the Muppet Club. What happened in the club was very simple: the children did some sewing and some cooking and played a 'running around' game.

Kay thought she had better visit it and turned up at the club's sixth session. She was astounded. Children who had been seen as unhappy, difficult and poor at relationships with adults and other children were blissfully happy: quiet, chatty, beaming.

Soon afterwards, she went to a meeting between the club-leaders and the children's teachers. There were some astonishing results. A child who had been so anxious that she wet herself whenever a teacher asked her to do anything had changed completely, becoming the cheekiest child in the club.

The mother of another, famously anti-school, came into school for the first time to talk things over – not to shout and swear at teachers. That child's reading levels had dramatically improved.

The next year, they ran six more clubs, led by students on placements, teachers and school welfare assistants. All of them seemed successful, producing dramatic changes in the social skills, general happiness and, above all, the self-confidence and self-esteem of many children.

Support from Other Studies

Meanwhile Kay had gone back to the library to read everything on file that mentioned clubs and groups for junior school age children. Why should ten weeks in a club have such dramatic effects? The work of two people seemed highly relevant.

Mortimer Schiffer[2]

In 1976 this American psychologist published an analysis of the way children in the 'latency' period between early childhood and adolescence have an 'instinctual social hunger' for acceptance by their own age-group.

Once this hunger was satisfied, and they succeeded in becoming an integrated part of a group of children their own age, they immediately became enormously receptive to learning all kinds of things, particularly social skills. Sympathetic adults, meeting their social and emotional needs, could have a disproportionate influence for a brief time.

I. Kolvin et al.[3]

As part of a wider study, Kolvin directed a project in Newcastle-upon-Tyne in the late 1970s which compared four matched groups of 7- to 8-year-old children considered 'at risk of maladjustment'.

One group of children took part in ten weekly playgroups, run by professionals. Another had five terms in a 'nurture group'. A third had three terms of parent and teacher counselling. Finally, a control group of similar children had no intervention at all. The researchers followed up the children twice, 18 months and three years after the intervention.

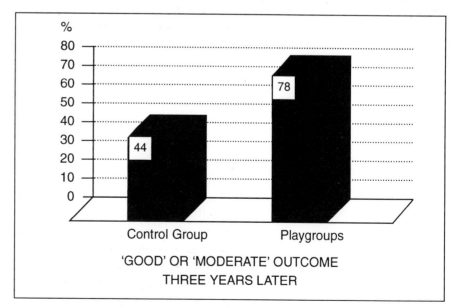

Figure 2 The Newcastle study of children 'at risk of maladjustment'

All types of intervention were more beneficial than no intervention. But some improvements were short-term. The intervention that had the most long-term impact was the cheapest and shortest: the one term, ten session playgroups. The benefits of the groups were not just immediately significant: the effects increased with time.

Three years after the experiment, the researchers found that 78 per cent of the playgroup children could be taken off the 'at risk' register, compared to 44 per cent of the control group.

By chance Kolvin's research was published just as the Hounslow project was coming to an end. At last, Kay felt that she had the basis of a successful model for low-cost preventive intervention to help children who were just about surviving in primary schools, but were at serious risks of later educational, social or emotional failure.

The key was to help them around the age of seven, eight or nine when they are open to help and change. By the time they reach adolescence, disaffected teenagers tend to have built walls between themselves and the rest of the world.

The Pyramid Model

By the end of the SSRC research a three-part preventive package had emerged:

- Screening children's all-round development
  All children are given one occasion in their primary careers when teachers consider their emotional, social, physical and educational development as a whole.
- Inter-professional co-operation
  The pooling of expertise and knowledge about individual children and families can support teachers and help them devise new strategies for some of the children.
- Activity group therapy
  The clubs would be affordable in any school because trained volunteers would run them.

Since the primary schools that had taken part in the action research in Hounslow were keen to continue the scheme, the local authority funded Kay to follow up the first group of 'club children', and compare their progress in their secondary schools with a group of similar children who had not had any intervention.

The results were very positive. Nearly all the children who had attended clubs were coping adequately in the mainstream, and their teachers expressed amazement that they had ever been singled out for special attention. Most of the control group had dropped out or were in special education. On the strength of this research, Hounslow agreed to extend the scheme to other schools.

With this backing, the Muppet Club project, named after the first club, flourished in Hounslow. It is still running there. One big breakthrough came when the West London Institute realised the project's potential for students on teacher training courses, and supplied a stream of excellent volunteers. Kay herself stayed with Hounslow, offering the system to an increasing numbers of schools until 1989.

Expansion

The time had come to publicise the scheme more widely. Several large children's charities were approached, but they had their own priorities and could not take the project on board.

So Kay started a new organisation with the sole purpose of developing preventive work with vulnerable children. The word 'Muppet' had developed unfortunate connotations so the 'Muppet Club' label was dropped. The new charity became The National Pyramid Trust.

In 1993 the Trust raised funds from the Department of Health and the Norman Trust to start pilot projects in Hillingdon and Bristol. A year later the BBC Children in Need fund sponsored a third pilot in Cardiff. The aim of the pilots was to see how successfully the scheme could be transplanted to different areas, and to develop the materials and systems needed to spread it nationally.

How the Scheme Works

Screening

First, each teacher of the selected year group (usually 7- to 9-year-olds in years 3 or 4) briefly considers all the children in their class using a check list to look at their attitudes, attendance and concerns about their general development and well-being.

This rough and ready 'screening' is not intended as a permanent record – it is simply a quick check to help busy teachers focus on those children who are not thriving. However, some schools are finding it a useful basis for monitoring the progress of the identified children.

Interdisciplinary Meeting

Next, teachers bring the list of the 'at risk' children to a meeting (known as the 'ID' meeting within the Trust) to which all the relevant professionals have been invited, including educational welfare officers, school nurses (and occasionally doctors), social workers, educational psychologists and school welfare assistants. Having been warned which children are to be discussed, they look up their records before the meeting. The idea is that the members of the school staff and the other professionals should pool their knowledge and experience. It is a rule that some positive intervention has to be agreed for every child mentioned.

Finally, the eight or ten children who seem particularly likely to benefit are offered the chance to join an after-school club, running one day a week for ten weeks. In making the selection the need to create a balanced, compatible group is borne in mind, as well as the needs of the individual children. The National Pyramid Trust has described suitable children as follows:

> The children who join the Pyramid clubs are not going to school with excitement or joy. They are likely to look back on school as a negative experience. They are not happy, and unhappiness tends to produce academic under-functioning.
>
> To a greater or less extent they are socially isolated, for reasons that may include personality traits, adverse home circumstances giving rise to tension and anxiety, learning difficulties and disabilities that set them apart from their peers. They often do not stand out as problem children. In this sense, one could call them the 'invisible children'.

Recruiting Volunteer Club-leaders

While the schools are going through the selection process, the local Pyramid project co-ordinator will have been finding and training volunteers to run the clubs. It is essential that volunteers are neutral adults (i.e. not parents or teachers of the children) so that the children are free from the pressures of their everyday lives and can develop new relationships and behaviours.

There are several possible sources of volunteers. Colleges and universities, training future professionals who want to work with children, such as student teachers, social workers, health workers, psychologists, and care workers, provide a steady flow of excellent volunteers.

The volunteers have about eight hours' training, covering the theory behind the clubs and practical ideas for running them. They receive on-going support from their NPT co-ordinator throughout the life of the club.

Once the club gets going the volunteer leaders endeavour to create a group ethos which offers children the four crucial ingredients for healthy child development, identified by Dr Mia Kellmer Pringle, the famous authority on children, in her classic book: 'The Needs of Children'.[4]

- praise and recognition
- love and security
- new experiences
- responsibility

Whenever possible the volunteers walk the children home, providing an extra opportunity for talking and building relationships. In the course of its short life each club goes on one outing, and ends with a good-bye party. Apart from that, what happens is up to the volunteers and the children.

Many students welcome a chance to work with children in an informal way, with plenty of time to get to know them and hear about their lives, families and opinions. The colleges also value the work: several have incorporated Pyramid club leadership into a module within a course of study.

Feedback

Towards the end of the club session another ID meeting is convened to which volunteers are invited. All the professionals who were involved in the selection are invited back to hear what the volunteers have learnt from observing children's development in the club. They also review the progress of children mentioned at the original selection meeting who did not attend clubs, and report back on the results of the strategies that were agreed.

If the aims of the scheme are achieved, everyone benefits.

- Professionals share their knowledge and experience, acquire new insights about individual children and combine to offer them (and their teachers) support. Relationships formed at the ID meetings oil the wheels of co-operation for times of crisis.
- Support agency workers such as nurses, social workers or psychologists are alerted to children at an early stage, when a little preventive effort may avoid a lot of expensive work later on. Furthermore it informs their existing work with families.
- Teachers and schools get a chance to focus on the more 'invisible' problems of children and to devise strategies to resolve them.

- Volunteer club-leaders learn a great deal about children, as well as having the satisfaction of boosting the confidence and self-image of the club members. They take responsibility for their own project and depend on teamwork for success.
- Finally, the children in the club are given an experience that they will enjoy and which, for some, can transform their lives.

CHAPTER 2

Pyramid in Action

This section is based on visits and conversations in two of the Pyramid pilot projects in the summer of 1995 when they were in their second year. Ten schools were involved in each area. Meetings and club sessions were attended in four schools, two in each area, and feedback was gained from some other schools.

The Selection Meeting

The large junior school with a richly multi-ethnic population and a high proportion of children with special needs was running its Pyramid project in some style. It was the second year that the school had taken part in the scheme, and it all went very smoothly. The deputy head chaired the meeting to review all those children in Year 3 (7- to 8-year-olds) who were causing their teachers some concern, and to select ten of them for a Pyramid club. There was a good turn-out of professionals. The school nurse, educational welfare officer and educational psychologist were all there.

The three Year 3 teachers had considered the children in their class as all-round individuals. They used a check-list, designed to be a 'trigger for action', which can be completed quickly. It covers physical development and personal adjustment, including relations with other children.

Schools have disagreed about the usefulness of this check-list. Most teachers have welcomed it, and seen it as a useful prompt to consider characteristics of those children who don't show up as having severe problems in the normal professional business of teaching and assessment in large classes. Some find it time-consuming and say it tells them nothing they did not know. A third group say that after initial doubts it proved worthwhile.

The teachers at the meeting were able to express their feelings and anxieties about the problems children in their classes were experiencing – problems which might seem fairly minor at this stage, but which they recognised might develop into a serious problem later on.

The other professionals at the meeting made helpful contributions to the discussions. The educational welfare officer used her knowledge about a

```
┌─────────────────────────────────────────────────┐
│                   CHECK-LIST                      │
│                                                   │
│  Does the child:                                  │
│  ● relate appropriately to peers?                 │
│  ● enjoy working with others?                     │
│  ● enjoy playing with others?                     │
│  ● relate appropriately to adults?                │
│  ● concentrate on tasks till completed?           │
│  ● accept help where necessary?                   │
│  ● adapt easily and with confidence to new situations? │
│                                                   │
│  Is s/he:                                         │
│  ● accepted by peers?                             │
│  ● happy?                                         │
│  ● energetic?                                     │
│  ● well motivated?                                │
│                                                   │
│  Is there a problem with:                         │
│  ● vision?  hearing?  mobility?  speech?  other?  │
│  ● does the child complain of aches and pains?    │
│                                                   │
└─────────────────────────────────────────────────┘
```

Part of the selection check-list, with questions requiring a simple yes/no.

child's older siblings to suggest how the school might help and support the mother more effectively.

The educational psychologist advised on the children's suitability for the Pyramid club and discussed other strategies to meet needs that were being suggested. She undertook to investigate two or three children further and to suggest ways teachers could tackle behaviour and other problems.

The meeting went on for nearly two hours. Teachers and the deputy head discussed ways of approaching some parents to tell them of teacher's concerns and to try to devise joint strategies with the parents.

The Pyramid project co-ordinator took careful notes about all the children discussed and the action agreed. She suggested the types of child likely to benefit most from the club. The aim was to have a balance of girls and boys, a good ethnic mix, and to exclude children who were known to be very disruptive. The meeting ended with ten children selected for the club.

Profiles of some of the children

Rachel

Described by her teacher as a 'lovely little girl who finds it hard to make relationships with other children and has no friends'. She had considerable problems at home and was on the social services child protection register. 'The fun aspect of the club could be just what she needs,' said her teacher.

Kulvinder

She lacked all confidence in her ability, refused to eat and often said that she wanted to die. Her mother was trying hard, taking her to out-of-school activities, but it was not apparently having much effect. The educational psychologist thought the problems sounded a bit too deep-seated to be tackled by the Pyramid club and undertook to investigate – but said, 'Let's try the club first.'

Manjit

A sad and lonely child. None of the other children liked her and she'd taken to stealing sweets.

Peter

An attention-seeker, with poor concentration, speaking and listening skills. At times he seemed very streetwise, but he was twitchy, difficult and ill at ease with other children.

Daniel

He only answered in class when he was sure he had the right answer and hated discussing his work. He was picked on in the playground, and his parents seemed very over-protective.

Sudeep

His home life revolved round the temple. At school he was way behind academically, his self-esteem was rock bottom and he seemed rude and stupid. Unsurprisingly, he had no friends.

Lee

He had a speech problem and other children had no time for him. He could be disruptive and he had no friends or much social life in or out of school.

The meeting was impressive to an outsider – providing a real insight into the kind of problems primary children bring with them to school, and into a good school's efforts to support them and their parents.

The assembled professionals' collective knowledge about children and their families was remarkable and, in this school, it was being used in sympathetic and constructive ways, with the needs and rights of children and parents well in mind. All those present said that they had valued this rare chance to share their knowledge and to discuss ways of helping children.

All three Pyramid selection meetings attended were successful. As one head in another school put it, 'We're setting aside quality time to discuss children who don't get time otherwise.'

At this meeting he emphasised that the project's aim was to do something for *every* child causing concern, to support the class teachers with positive action and to deepen their understanding of each child.

Not all Pyramid selection meetings follow the model as well as these. Involving outside professionals is not easy. Sometimes the educational psychologists and education welfare officers can't or won't attend the meetings. Often, these days, the payment for the educational psychologist's time has to come out of hard-pressed school budgets, and children who are more disruptive or have more severe and visible learning problems take up more than the budget available.

Even when they do attend, professionals are not always made to feel welcome and involved. 'I'm here because I was told to be,' said an educational psychologist, rather crossly, at one meeting, making very little further contribution. Since this school had already more or less decided which children were going to be in the club and what to do about other children causing concern, this particular meeting was, in any case, not as appropriate for outsiders as the others.

In schools running the project for the first time, teachers can be understandably suspicious about the whole thing. In one meeting a teacher tended to ramble on a bit, complaining about parents rather than searching for ways to support them. At another there were slightly hostile questions from a young class teacher. He asked what on earth could a club run by student volunteers for ten weeks achieve and how could they present the scheme to parents without them feeling their child has been stigmatised?

Where the project was running for a second year, these questions seem to have evaporated. Several children who went to the club the previous year had benefited, and the benefits had lasted.

'The scheme boosted children's confidence and their ability to relate to their peers, make friends, and join in, and the changes seemed to stick,' said one head teacher.

Involving parents

Most schools simply informed parents that there was an opportunity for their child to join the club if parents were agreeable, emphasising that they thought the child would benefit (see p. 12). Very few parents asked further questions.

Training the Volunteer Club-leaders

The blueprint for training volunteers to run Pyramid clubs calls for four two-hour sessions.

Session one

gives a general introduction to the scheme and focuses on the importance of group experiences. The volunteers discuss their own experience of groups. They are given a brief introduction to group work theory and to some practical techniques for getting groups going in the early stages.

Session two

concentrates on the clubs, their purpose and the kinds of activities that work well with children. The volunteers try out some of the activities themselves and are given guidelines and check-lists to help them plan the club sessions.

Session three

goes into more detail about the clubs and the typical stages they go through. It also gets the volunteers to anticipate situations and behaviour that may be difficult to handle, and strategies for dealing with these are discussed

Session four

deals with the nuts and bolts – the contract the leaders are entering into, health and safety, child protection issues and insurance. Volunteers discuss potential problems when taking children home, relations with parents, planning, and how to say good-bye at the last session of the club – usually a very sad time for both children and volunteers.

MODEL LETTER

Dear Parents

Trained volunteers from .... are setting up an activity group for a small number of children. It is planned to do a variety of creative activities including some local visits and to give the group an opportunity to develop their social and communication skills. I am delighted that we are able to offer this place and wish it was available for a larger number of children.

The groups will be directly after school and at ...., once a week for ten weeks. Sessions will be for about an hour and a half and the programme will probably begin on .... and end on .... The children in the group will be brought home by the students at the end of each session.

I do hope that you will give your permission for .... to join the group and ask that you let me know by returning the slip below. If you would like to hear more about this opportunity please contact me.

To make sure that our records are up to date would you please give below, your address, telephone number and the name, address and telephone number of a neighbour/relative whom we could contact in an emergency.

Yours sincerely

_____

I am/am not willing for .... to join the activity group, starting on .... , and to be brought home by the Club Leader.

A. Home Address ....
....Tel. no. ....

B. Name of neighbour/relative
....
Home Address ....
....   Tel. no. ....

Any additional information, including medical, the leaders should have.

Signed ....

A Training Session in Practice

The training session visited had to compress all four sessions into one long day, for reasons outside the Pyramid co-ordinator's control. The shortened course was still effective because the volunteers were all more than halfway through a postgraduate teacher training course and, therefore, had good experience of children and schools.

The day was led by the local Pyramid Trust co-ordinator, a former primary head teacher. She herself had worked in a club the previous year. She brought along another volunteer who had run a club, so between them they could offer plenty of first-hand experience to the new club-leaders.

Establishing Group Identity

Volunteers started the session as they might well start a club, wearing brightly decorated name badges they had made. They talked about why they were interested in the project.

'I want to develop a more rounded idea of children – to see them in a different light than you do as a teacher,' said one.

Another was attracted by 'the confidence-boosting aspect, which is so important at an early age'.

Figure 3 Building a relationship of trust

The co-ordinator introduced the theory and research behind this method of tackling low self-esteem emphasising the techniques for building group ethos:

'Getting children going as a *group* is what makes it work.'

She explained that the clubs can give children a happy experience of getting along with their peers in a safe place, with plenty of adults around, before they become too fixed in their image of themselves as outsiders. The students discussed their own happy experiences of being in a group, and what it was that they had enjoyed.

Several agreed that they themselves would benefit as well as the children.

'We'll learn more about special needs and it will be good to learn more about primary schools and their problems, and children at that stage.'

Responsibility and Commitment

The co-ordinator stressed the responsibility of the job and the commitment needed. It was important to be there early, to be ready when the children arrive, to get children home safely and to keep brief records of what had happened. It was also important to leave any explaining about why children had been picked for clubs to the school: 'They thought you'd enjoy it a lot,' was usually an answer children found perfectly satisfactory.

Building up Group Solidarity
(Extract from the NPT Handbook by Kay FitzHerbert [5])

In activity group therapy two ingredients are essential: belonging to a secure group of one's peers and having positive experience in that setting. Your first task as a leader is therefore to manipulate the eight or ten individuals presented to you at your first session into their very own unique club or secret society. Here are some ideas that previous leaders have used successfully:

- Getting the children to choose a name for their club with an accompanying logo, motto, coat-of-arms, secret code-word or handshake.
- Making everyone a badge of the club's logo out of materials that have ranged from cardboard and bread dough to felt and potter's clay.
- Inventing a special ritual that the whole group has to enact every week.
- Designing an elaborate register for every child to tick on arriving for the club session.

- Compiling individual club ID cards, passports or folders for each member.

You can spend many happy sessions on this task, starting out by asking everyone to fill out a nice ego-boosting questionnaire on their personal details for the ID card, taking a photograph, decorating a folder or wallet with the club symbol to put everything else in etc. Individual folders are actually quite useful for collecting all the bits and pieces that accumulate for each child during the club and for taking home at the end as a souvenir.

- Buying a cheap, plain mug for each child, letting everyone paint on their names and the club emblem, using the mugs for drinks for the duration of the club and letting them be taken home at the end, full of sweets.
- Painting a large, communal banner of the club emblem. (This wasn't attempted before the leaders were confident that the group had achieved the necessary degree of co-operation, something like halfway through the life of the club.)

In practice, most games and craft activities can be adapted to contribute to group cohesion. There is no need to rush; it's not a 'one-off' process. You can carry on emphasising the solidarity theme right to the last session.

The Four Stages of a Club

These are:

forming
storming
performing
mourning

Most clubs start nervously, followed by a difficult patch while some children test the limits of acceptable behaviour. Then they usually settle down and the club runs more easily and productively. The ending of a club can be an unhappy experience for the children who are often sad or angry that the club is finishing. Each stage requires different activities.

The leaders were told it was a good idea to find a way of reminding children of the duration of the club each week – maybe with some version of an advent calendar to mark off each session.

The clubs are designed to have their own rhythm. A key part of the Pyramid project is that every club should have an outing about halfway through its life, with the children involved in choosing where they go. The students were told that the outing is often the moment when the group really gels and starts 'performing'. All clubs must end on a high note with a good-bye party, including special food and games, and some ceremony, such as the presentation of certificates.

Outings
(Extract from the NPT Handbook by Kay FitzHerbert)

Outings can have a miraculous effect on a club; being together in your clubroom every week is one thing, but being out in the world as a united group in a world of strangers is altogether different and does wonders for raising group consciousness. This goes as much for a local trip to the swimming baths or the park in one of the ordinary club sessions as for an exciting all-day outing undertaken at the week-end or at half-term.

If the expedition is a full-scale one to somewhere special where the children have never been before, with picnics and a mini-bus thrown in, it usually becomes the club's most memorable experience and is talked about for ever afterwards. Though it is best not undertaken in the first few weeks, before at least some group rapport has been established, it could be the catalyst which gels the children into a real unit. The precise destination of the outing is of secondary importance; all the ones listed below have been successfully undertaken by Hounslow groups:

swimming (always brilliantly successful)   skating
horse-riding   Chessington Zoo
Thorpe Park   McDonald's
'The Sights of London' (by public transport!) Brighton
picnics in the park followed by cricket   Heathrow Airport
carol singing (£5 raised for Kampuchea)

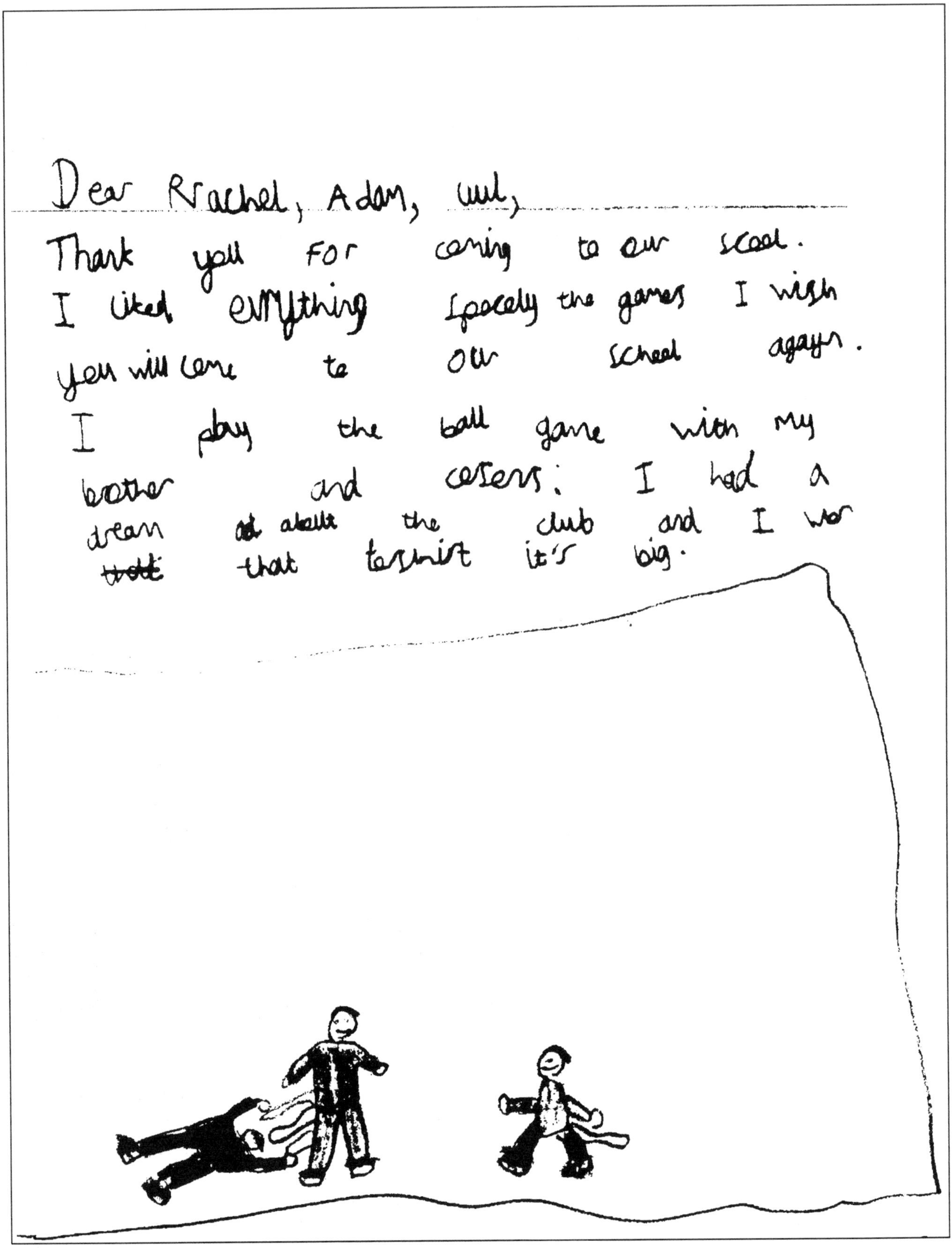

Dear Rrachel, Adam, uul,

Thank you for coming to our scool. I liked evrything spacely the games I wish you will come to our scheel agayn. I play the ball game with my brother and cosens. I had a drean about the club and I wor that tennist it's big.

Figure 4 A letter of appreciation from a club member

Figure 5 A Club Outing

Some Techniques and Activities

Suggestions were made, discussed and some were practised by the volunteers:

- Ice-breaking games such as sitting in a circle throwing a ball to one other and naming the person to whom it was thrown, could be used to get to know the children at the beginning of the club.

Figure 6 Circle Time

- The importance of names was emphasised: children love making things with their names on them, such as mugs or T-shirts, and choosing a name for their club at the first session. They should also decide a few rules – preferably dos rather than don'ts.
- Cooking – or at least assembling food if there is no scope for cooking – is always a favourite. The volunteers had a good time on the training day, using various spreads on biscuits with amazing decorative effects – all of which were possible for children.

- Active games, such as: 'Simon Says' or versions of tig; craft activities; playing with kites and parachutes; communication games with codes; quiet Circle Times where the children and volunteers shared feelings and opinions – all these had proved successful in clubs.

Figure 7 Indoor 'tig'

The Nuts and Bolts

The training day ended by discussing:

- child protection issues and routines;
- budgets – from the time the scheme began in Hounslow until 1995, each club had only £80 or £10 per child to spend; the recommended amount is now about £15 per head.

Students were reminded of the importance of:

- knowing children's addresses and telephone numbers, who to contact in the school, what to do if there was an accident and the importance of checking out car insurance if the volunteers were driving children home;
- being clear which member of the team would handle which responsibility – money, transport, etc.;
- sorting out who would lead the main activity, who would cope with dissenters and who would watch for children who needed individual attention.

The volunteers tried to foresee problems and devise strategies to deal with them. They discussed fights, racism or name-calling; how to respond when a child says, 'I'm off,' and runs out; or when they find no one is home to receive a child.

It was a packed day's work. But the volunteers carried home a file of practical ideas and material, and they had the reassurance that the co-ordinator would be on hand throughout the life of the clubs to offer help and advice. Moreover, since the volunteers were all at college together there were good opportunities for the club leaders to meet and plan. One of the clubs visited was run by students from this session who showed that the training day preparation led to some very good, well-planned work with children.

Club Case Studies

Club One

The school was in an outer city, mainly white working-class area with relatively few 'problem' families, but with more than its share of difficult children and children with special needs.

Chris, Caroline and Jo, the three club-leaders, were all students at the local university doing a graduate secondary school teacher training course. Chris and Caroline were mature students. Both had young children of their own, and their experience contributed to the relaxed atmosphere of the club. Jo had worked with adolescents in a secure unit and wanted to explore possibilities for preventive work with younger children.

The club, called 'The Terrible Kids' by the children, was in its second session. The 7- and 8-year-olds hadn't yet gelled as a group. The club took place in a room next to the hall and it was difficult to get Lloyd and Kevin, who were noisily kicking a football in the hall, to come and settle down.

But the volunteers seemed to have chosen an ideal activity to soothe even hyperactive boys who seemed visibly allergic to structured activity or girls. They'd brought along some home-made playdough.

Soon all the children were happily sitting round the table, some making elaborate models. One girl carefully produced a whole playdough meal on a plate, with hamburger, tomatoes and peas. The boys (particularly Lloyd and Kevin) simply bashed the dough into crude shapes, but they did it in a contented and absorbed way.

After about ten minutes, concentration wavered and the boys began smashing up each others' models and were moving in on those of the girls. The volunteers moved them smartly into the hall where Caroline led a drama session.

It took a few minutes to get all the children interested in pretending they were lying on a hot beach – but in the end they all joined in. Soon they were calm and co-operative enough for a vigorous tig-style game, rushing around with a shark chasing swimmers in the sea.

Then it was time for a snack and talk. The volunteers had brought along biscuits and drinks and, as the children ate, they discussed club rules that they'd started to make up the previous week.

Figure 8 Painting together

'No-one shows off', was thought to be a good idea, as was 'No fighting'. The club leaders asked for some dos as well as the don'ts. They were pleased to get:

'Make sure everyone is happy'

'Use nice words'

'Play games properly'

'Everybody share everything, including clearing up'

Activities and Games from the Bristol Pyramid Clubs

Activities

name badges	box-decorating	fantasy film – flowers/bees
cooking	masks	treasure island from scrap
growing cress	mug-painting	octopus hand-painting
posters	bubble painting	party hats
'get well' cards	dough sculpture	T-shirt designs
kites	sock puppets	membership cards
fimo modelling	marbling	printing with vegetables

Games

board games	Please Mr Crocodile	circle games, e.g. Passing the Keys
Railway Stations	Stuck in the Mud	
Duck/Duck/Goose	Chair Name Game	Pass the Parcel (with forfeits)
Sleeping Lions	Zip/Zap/Bong	
Hum/Yell	parachute games	Fruit Salad
ball games		Hide and Seek

Trips

Bristol Zoo	Planet Kids	Bath Adventure Playground
horse-riding	Skate Attack	Windmill City Farm visit
picnics	Ashton Court	

Figure 9 Hide and seek

The most difficult part of the session was getting all the children home, as they lived over a fairly wide area; even with a car it took a long time. In the end the school asked parents to come and collect their children. This made the volunteers' lives easier. However, they and the children missed out on what many club-leaders and children find one of the most rewarding parts of the routine: going home together gives time to chat and provides the volunteers with an opportunity to see something of the children's homes.

A few weeks later, at its second to last session, the Terrible Kids had settled down nicely. By then the children had been taken on an outing to a city farm where even boys who considered themselves really hard, and who started by throwing stones at the animals, calmed down and finally melted completely when they bottle-fed some lambs.

Back at school in the ninth club session, the volunteers had brought colourful lengths of material they'd found at the local scrap store; the children had a wonderful time making the material billow as they danced.

Then they planned their good-bye party for the next week, and made some party hats. The girls rapidly settled to making themselves lavishly decorated crowns, and Chris managed to get the boys settled almost as quickly when she suggested pirate hats with skulls and crossbones.

Club Two

The second session of this very different club in a much more deprived area (a teacher said the local street was known as 'Terror Avenue') went less smoothly. Some of the children tended to wander about, outdoor games were a bit of a shambles and there were quite a lot of tears and complaints such as, 'He's picking on me, Miss.'

There were some problems with children who wanted to take themselves home at the end of the session: the leaders had to be very firm that it was part of their responsibility to go with the children.

But by the penultimate session of this club there were marked changes. Anthony, who'd been weepy and miserable at the beginning, was now showing distinct leadership qualities – 'Come *on* everybody'. Dane, one of the more rackety boys, said to Susie, a shy little girl, 'I missed you when you was away.'

The boys who'd complained about being taken home were now vying with the others to be the last one to be dropped off home: they wanted the extra time on their own with the leaders.

Club Three

This was visited at the height of the 'storming' stage. The volunteers coped brilliantly, getting children going on noisy jumping and stamping games, and the 'Hokey Cokey', then calming them down with a game of Chinese Whispers, before having a session about club rules. 'Have fun,' someone suggested. 'That's not a rule,' said a little girl. Other suggestions included:

'Make friends'

'If you're sad, tell someone'

'Everybody joins in'

My name is Mathew

I am 8 years old.

I have 3 brothers and 1 sisters.

My favourite food is Chicken and Beef Burgers

I like the Friendly Balloon Club because; I have lots of friends.

Figure 10 Friendly Balloon Club registration form

This club's final party session showed how much had been achieved. Party games such as Musical Chairs and Pass the Parcel were in full swing. There were balloons and an enormous tea, with children proudly using mugs they had decorated.

PYRAMID PROJECT

The Friendly Balloon Club Certificate

Awarded to :

Who for 10 weeks has been a valued member of the fun filled 'Friendly Balloon Club.'

WELL DONE!

Signed :

Figure 11 Friendly Balloon Club certificate of achievement

The volunteers handed out their certificates 'for special people' with fine ceremony and there were big hugs for the leaders.

'I wish we *never* had to leave the club,' said one little girl.

'*So* do I,' said a boy.

There's no such thing as a 'typical' Pyramid club. Of the four visited, two seemed to be running to a fairly tight structure with briskly-led activities such as 'Simon Says' and 'Follow My Leader', followed by more structured craft sessions and 'Circle Times' where volunteers and children shared news or feelings.

The other two were much more laid back. In one, the children and volunteers spent a lot of time outdoors in lovely summer weather. The leaders weren't too concerned about getting everyone to join in organised games and were relaxed when children wandered off to the edge of the field, as long as they were still in sight.

It seemed a bit fragmented and disorganised, but the approach created a lot of time for the leaders to chat to children in ones and twos and the children loved it.

Whatever their approach, all four clubs had at least one or two children whose teachers felt they had really come on dramatically during their ten weeks at the club. All the teachers commented on how much the children had enjoyed the club and how enthusiastic they were on club days.

Comments from Volunteers

'One big problem for many children with behaviour problems is that they don't know how to play with others. It was great to see them beginning to play happily, and to give them resources for entertaining themselves – it could have huge benefits for some children.'

'It was a really good experience, working with a small group, being able to concentrate on a few children and think about what was happening.'

'It's brought some of *us* out of our shells as well.'

'I knew the club was worthwhile when a child, described as shy and nervous, gave me a big hug!'

'Don't worry if the group is not going how you planned, as long as the kids are OK.'

'It's not a teaching experience; it doesn't matter if they don't learn anything new as long as they have a feeling of achievement.'

'Enjoy the club while it lasts because it is over very quickly.'

Feedback Meetings

The final stage of the Pyramid scheme is the feedback meeting, where the teachers and, ideally, the other professionals, meet the club-leaders and swap information about how the children responded and how they changed over the ten-week period.

At all three feedback meetings, the teachers were very impressed by the leaders' perceptive insights into children's behaviour and difficulties, and clearly intended to follow up the questions and suggestions from the volunteers.

In all the schools one or two children had made quite spectacular progress and most seemed noticeably happier for the experience. More than one teacher said, 'He (or she) is *smiling* much more.'

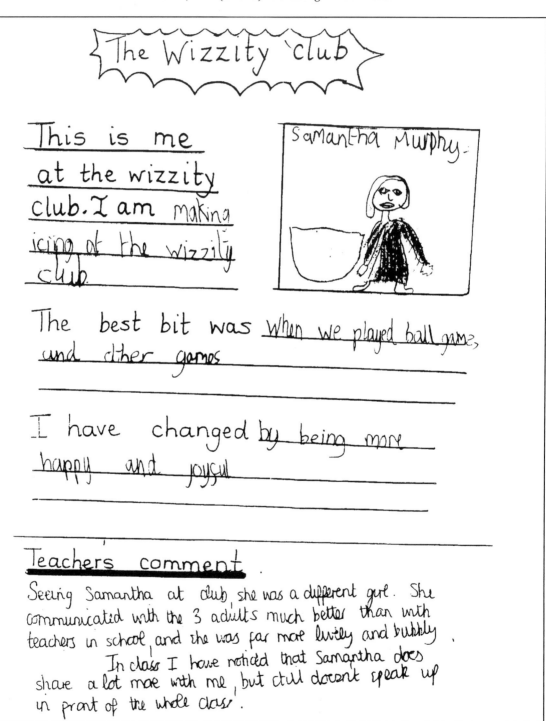

Figure 12

Some children who benefited

Peter

This 'streetwise' boy had started at the club by being very off-hand and difficult. But he'd gradually mellowed and begun to talk about his feelings. By the end he'd even held hands with one of the leaders on the way home. Both the club-leaders and his teacher thought this was a considerable breakthrough. His teacher reported he had been much calmer in school, working better and wanting to please.

Lee

Because of his speech problem, Lee had found the club difficult at first. He didn't want much to do with the others and found it hard to understand and accept that games had rules. Frustration had led to tantrums. The leaders thought they'd helped him to accept rules and play with others, and that he'd become much more integrated in the group.

His teacher said, 'I think it benefited him enormously – he enjoyed it and talked about it a lot. He's surrounded by adults at home and doesn't see other children much.'

Manjit

This child had been quite a problem in the club, disruptive and mean to other children. The leaders had tried to talk to her about it, asking how she could expect people to like her if she was nasty to them, but they felt they hadn't made much headway. However, her teacher said that she had seen a difference – and Manjit had stopped stealing sweets.

Julie

She had started off by being very negative and disruptive. But when the leaders told her that she would have to leave the club, she'd become much easier and nicer.

Neyma

This girl was the big success of her club. In the beginning she was really shy and withdrawn, but she ended up being mischievous and adventurous. Her teacher said, 'She's standing up for herself much better in class. She's really started taking the initiative.'

All the clubs had a child who, like Neyma, had changed markedly. Teachers said things like:

'He's speaking out much more';

'She's gained a lot of confidence and formed more friendships';

'She's smiling much more and taking pride in her work. She starts conversations now'.

One boy who'd caused a lot of trouble at the beginning of the club, not least by running down the street on the way home and calling the volunteer with him a pervert, became 'an angel' after the leaders had to threaten to throw him out of the club.

The Wizzity Club

This is me at the wizzity club. I am ~~doing~~ ~~playing~~ ~~hit~~ a ball ~~game~~.

Leanne Page

The best bit was when we went on the ~~ti~~ trip to the farm.

I have changed by being louder and having more Ideas to think about.

Teachers comment.

Leanne is still quite shy and timid and has quite a lot of time off because of illness.
   She always reported back to me about club and seemed an active member.

Figure 13

The Wizzity club

John Hoddinott

This is me at the wizzity club. I am holding a baby lam on our trip.

The best bit was looking at all the animals.

I have changed by playing at home.

Teacher's comment.

Getting more mature although there's still long way to go, but he's less ~~dp~~ reliant on others.

Figure 14

It was interesting that the threats of exclusion reported had all had good effects. It seems that even the most difficult and disruptive children were having a sufficiently good experience to make them want to continue. Only two children in all the pilot schools had finally had to be excluded from a club.

One father had taken his daughter out of one of the clubs visited, ostensibly because of 'all the swearing'. This was sad because the little girl enjoyed the club and the volunteers were dealing firmly with any swearing.

At the feedback meetings the leaders offered useful practical insights into children's problems. The teachers knew that one girl had a slight hearing problem but, in the small group of the club, the leaders had found it much worse than they had been led to expect; it was effectively cutting the child off from what was happening around her. The school immediately arranged for a check-up. Another child clearly didn't get enough to eat at home; she was often ravenously hungry and wanted to take biscuits back to share with her siblings. Again, the school decided they should tactfully try to follow this up.

All in all, both leaders and teachers seemed very pleased with the results. Three of the schools visited had more than 40 per cent of children with identified special educational needs. In such schools well-prepared volunteers could do invaluable work with children for whom the school had nothing much to offer, since the limited resources went to meet the needs of children with the most immediate and serious learning and behaviour problems.

One head said, 'The friendships children made in last year's club have continued; the effects don't drop away. They smile, they feel better about themselves, they're easier with the world around them.'

Figure 15 Feeding a lamb

Perhaps the biggest tribute to a club came from a father. To the leaders and his teacher, Tony seemed to have enjoyed the club but they didn't see any great breakthrough. He had needed a lot of reassurance, tending to sit on one side and bursting into tears a lot. By the end he had begun to make friends and had started joining in.

But to his father, the change had been dramatic. 'He thoroughly enjoyed himself, and he is *much* more confident now about dealing with other children and adults. He goes out and about on his bike now – it's really brought him out of himself. He's a different little boy, really.'

How children changed

B (girl)

At the beginning of the year she didn't speak and was cold and withdrawn towards her teacher. In the club she would not join in Circle Time initially but gradually she began to confide in the leaders, join in the games and enjoy herself with increasing confidence. A bit of a 'tomboy', she enjoyed playing with the boys.

In class her work increased dramatically – she is now 'beavering away' and this has coincided with her time in the club. She is warmer and more open and made a card for her teacher saying 'I love you'.

T (girl)

T was from an Asian family in a white working-class area and her mother was very concerned about the rough neighbourhood, telling T not to make friends in class. T attended the club *every* week – if there had been the slightest parental concern she would have been withdrawn.

Although she was very quiet on the trip and in later sessions she joined in more and ran around. T said she enjoyed playing: 'I'd never played like that before.'

Her mother was very positive about the club and invited the club leaders in for tea.

M (boy)

Quite immature, he clung to adults. He irritated the other children and was disliked and a bit bullied by them.

In the club the other children welcomed him much more, opening up to him. When the group was playing with the parachute, M withdrew, but when he rejoined the group they all cheered.

In school he wrote that he didn't know how to get on with other children and in the first week of the club one of the boys said, 'No one likes M,' but by the end of the club this same boy had invited M home for tea.

The head said even a small gain is quite exceptional for M (he transferred from another school because of bullying). His mother was close to tears at how happy he is now in school.

CHAPTER 3

Evaluation

The big question asked by everyone is: can the Pyramid scheme possibly work? Can ten 90-minute sessions, run by volunteers after eight hours of training, possibly alter children's long-term life chances?

Research Studies

There have been two small-scale research studies that both produced positive, though not conclusive, results.

Study One

In 1984, after the government's Social Science Research Council had funded a pilot scheme, Hounslow employed Kay FitzHerbert to follow a group of 34 children who had been to clubs through to their third year of secondary school.

As a control group she followed a group of 22 slightly older children from the same schools as the club children. They had been identified as 'at risk' in the same way as the experimental group, but had received no intervention.

The study[6] was small-scale and *ad hoc*, but its results were striking. By their third year of secondary school:

- 27 of the club children (about four-fifths) were either doing well academically or socially in the mainstream, or, if their academic achievements were low, were settled in and working well.
- of those who were still isolated and teased, most seemed to be coping with remarkable resilience.

In contrast:

- only five children from the control group were still in their secondary schools;
- nine had been sent on to boarding schools or special units;
- five were chronic non-attenders;
- three of the five who did turn up at school showed severe emotional or behaviour problems.

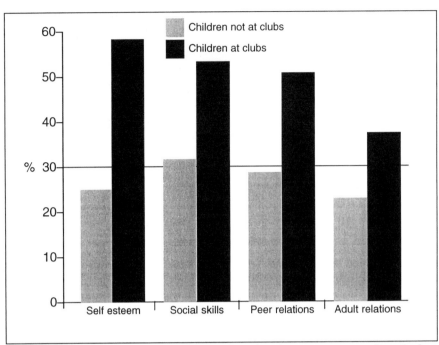

Figure 16 Percentages of children showing improvement after their clubs in 1995

Study Two

The second evaluation by T. C. Skinner,[7] from the Psychology Department of the University of Surrey, took place in 1995. After the clubs in the two pilot projects had finished, teachers were asked to fill in forms about all the children whose names had come up at the first screening meetings that year. Teachers from thirteen schools filled in evaluations for 148 children: 110 were for children who had attended clubs, and 38 for children who had not been selected for clubs.

Teachers were asked to assess the children's academic progress in reading, writing, spelling and maths as well as any changes in their social and emotional development. They reported on changes in self-esteem, social skills, relations with other children and with adults.

- *Self-esteem*
  The most significant difference between the club-goers and non-club-goers was the improvement in the self-esteem of the club children. Teachers reported that the self-esteem of 57 per cent of the club-goers had improved, compared with 24 per cent of non-club-goers.

- *Social skills*
  Club-going children had also improved their social skills, their relationships with peers, and their relationships with adults more than the other children, though these findings were less significant statistically.

- *Academic improvement*
  The club children had made significantly more progress in writing – an unexpected outcome. Perhaps improved social and emotional well-being improves children's ability to express their thoughts on paper. Or it may be that, as one primary head teacher put it, 'The club gave them the self-confidence to do well academically.'

Figure 17 New experiences

There was quite a big variation between the results in different clubs. Some were much more effective than others. The data from this evaluation could not identify the special ingredients of the most successful clubs. The Trust is planning to continue evaluating results, and in particular to collect more information from leaders about the activities in their clubs, to try to identify the factors that made for the best results.

So evaluation to date suggests that the Pyramid scheme works for large numbers of children. Furthermore, the results of these small-scale attempts at evaluation chime well with Kolvin's much larger project in Newcastle-upon-Tyne (see pages 3/4). The follow-up research in Hounslow also supports Kolvin's crucial findings that the effects of short-term therapeutic groups for pre-adolescent children increase with time. Kay FitzHerbert believes that even in cases where there is no immediate improvement, the clubs may provide, as it were, a slow-release fertiliser which promotes future growth.

It will take a larger scale, longitudinal study to provide conclusive data. At the time of writing, the National Pyramid Trust is discussing such a study with the University of Surrey which it hopes to start in 1997.

Anecdotal Evidence

There is also a great deal of anecdotal evidence from parents, teachers and the children themselves that confirms the results of research so far, showing the scheme's very positive results for many children, at least in the short-term.

For the past two years, the local Pyramid co-ordinators of the pilot schemes have sent questionnaires to parents and talked to parents, teachers and children once the clubs have finished. The results are worth quoting at some length, since they help to confirm the theory behind the Pyramid clubs.

Parents

Virtually all the parents reported that their child had enjoyed the club. Many made positive comments about the effects.

'He has become more talkative and willing to go outside to play.'

'It's made her mix better with people.'

'He's learned how to get on with other children better, and listen when someone is talking to him.'

'She was shy before, she seems different now.'

What did s/he particularly enjoy?

I think he enjoyed the feeling of 'belonging', and was quite proud of the fact that his choice of name 'The Lion Kings' was picked. The boy that came home on weds eves. was so different from the boy that comes home from school.

How do you think your child has benefitted from the club?

Yes, when D____ returned from the club he seemed extremely enthusiastic and full of beans. he couldn't wait to tell me all about it. He has also become more talkative and willing to go outside to play.

Are there any other comments you would like to add?

I would like to thank both Anna-Lee and Anne for what must have been extremely hard work on occasion. I just wish that he had started much earlier. Maybe his self-confidence may have helped him to cope better with the bullying that he has suffered. PLEASE KEEP IT UP! to help other children like D____.

Figure 18 Parent's evaluation of their child's Pyramid club

Several parents said their child had developed more self-confidence and enthusiasm for doing things. Parents found that their boys and girls had become:

'More out-going.'

'More independent.'

'More outspoken, a bit cheeky, really.'

'More mouthy, so it has obviously boosted her confidence.'

Several also mentioned that their children were happier about school.

'I think she enjoyed the feeling of belonging.'

The value of providing a neutral, non-judgemental environment was acknowledged by one parent:

'He enjoyed the adult company, where he wasn't judged all the time which I'm afraid we did in the past.'

Teachers

The children's teachers had similar views:

'He's more sociable, more amenable.'

'She wants to please more now.'

'He has become friendlier and more respectful of other children.'

'Before she was always off school, and always whingeing. Her attendance and her attitude have improved.'

'He no longer complains of headaches and tummy aches, and doesn't cry any more.'

'Others no longer tease her. If they do she's more assertive and answers them back.'

'His confidence has improved. His work has come on by leaps and bounds and he will now have a go at writing on his own.'

One head teacher made an important point: 'Once children have been identified, even before they attend a club, they are no longer invisible because we are aware of their needs.'

The schools visited in 1995 and the children and parents interviewed confirmed these responses. 'She can take criticism now,' said the teacher of one child, adding, 'She's never in the medical room any more.' Another child, who had been described at the first selection meeting as 'unhappy and afraid of getting things wrong', had completely changed. 'She's much happier and jollier, smiling and laughing most of the time,' said her teacher. 'She's more willing to contribute in class. Her parents are more involved.'

The last point is one often brought up by teachers. Several parents, who had previously been quite hostile towards the school, resisting the school's attempt to discuss their children's progress or behaviour, seemed to have changed their attitude after the child had attended a Pyramid club. Perhaps they realised that their child had had an enjoyable experience of school for a change, or that the school was doing something positive.

Teachers reported that the effects had been 'extraordinary', or 'dramatic' for one or two children in virtually all the clubs. 'It's hard to grasp why something so simple is so significant,' said one special needs co-ordinator.

Children

When you talk to children about the clubs, they all say they are 'fun', 'really good'. The names they give their clubs show their attitude: they call them 'The Fun Club', 'The Really Wicked Club', 'The Friday Club' (which met on Wednesdays).

Club Names chosen by the children		
Wacky Joke Club	Can't Remember Club	The Funky Fun Club
Animal Club	Dog and Cat Club	The Special Club
Sharky Club	Wizz Bang Fizz Club	The Action Club
The Crazy Club	The Giggsy Club	The Friendly Balloon Club
The Monster Club	The Good Friends Club	The Cool Kids

'We had fun. When I go home I don't have fun. It was exciting,' said one girl.

'You have a fun time and once you get to know the leaders it gets funner and funner,' said a boy.

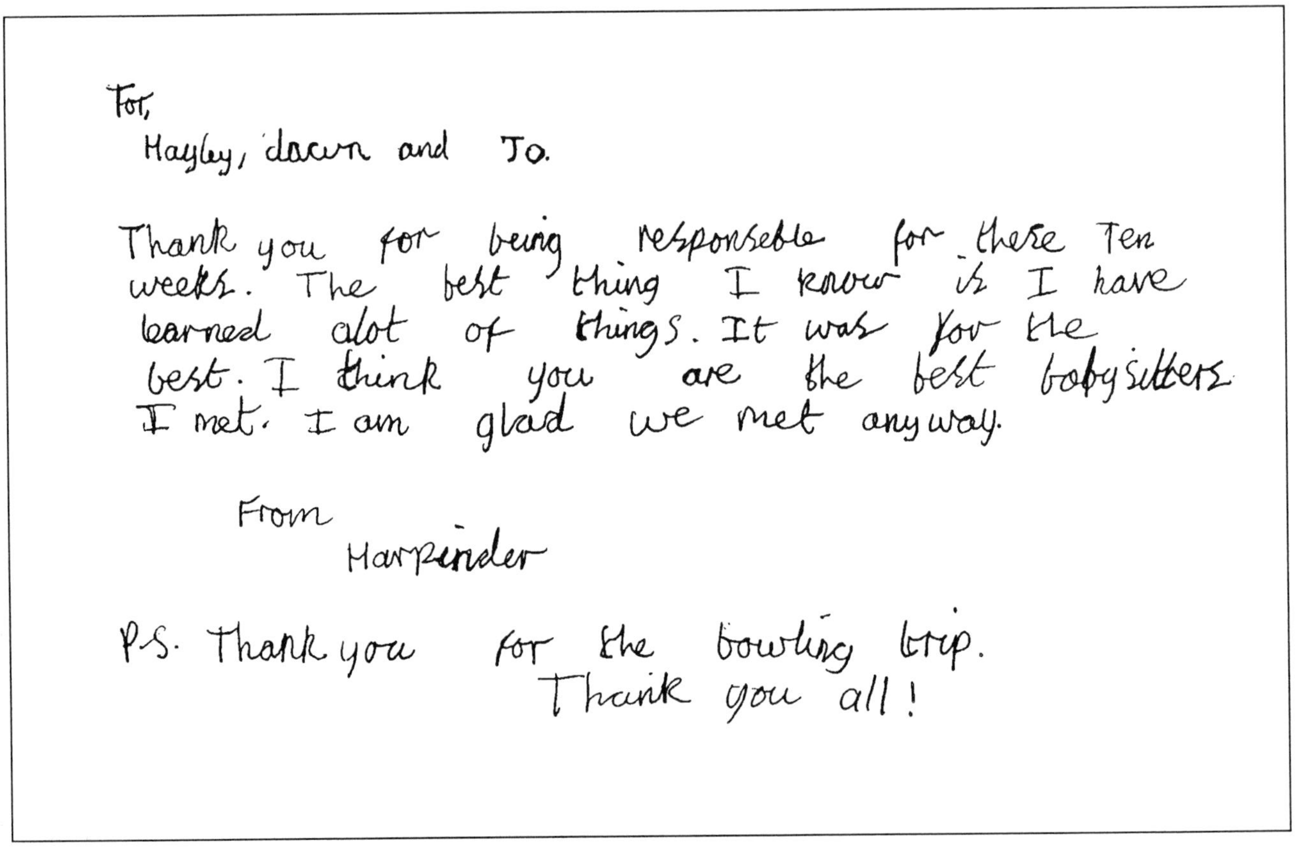

For,
Hayley, dawn and Jo.

Thank you for being responseble for these Ten weeks. The best thing I know is I have learned alot of things. It was for the best. I think you are the best baby sitters I met. I am glad we met anyway.

From
Harpinder

P.S. Thank you for the bowling trip.
Thank you all!

Figure 19 Unsolicited appreciation

'I have changed by being louder and having more ideas to think about,' said another.

'I wish it could have gone on for ever,' was a wish expressed by several children.

St John Loyld's
Cemaes cres
Rumney
Cardiff

Dear students,
Thank you for the food, and the chocolate, the game tatking about our selves.
The trip was good but it was cold I enjoyed it
Love from
Ben
xxx

Figure 20 Response from The Wizzity Club

Some children showed greater insight:

'I learned to be good, to be friends and to be great with everyone.'

'Now I can be happy with other people, they like me.'

'I learned to be friends with other children, and share stuff, and make stuff for them.'

Or, simply and starkly: 'I like myself now.'

Figure 21 Working together

None of this anecdotal evidence shows that the children's new spirit and self-confidence will last. But several primary heads in schools where the project had run for two years, maintain that the effects do seem to have lasted.

For example, two girls who did not get on at all well with other children made friends with each other, and both were still doing very well a year later. So was a very withdrawn child who came 'right out of her shell' after the club – and stayed out.

'The most quiet and withdrawn children become more socially equal with the class. They develop a new attitude: "I am worthy; I count; I can communicate",' said a head.

The Schools' Response

A primary school inspector who was instrumental in introducing the scheme in Hillingdon said, 'The biggest indicator of its success is the fact that highly critical and aware schools all wanted to go on with it for a second and third year. And they tell me they have identified some dramatic changes in some children.' By the summer of 1996 every one of the 42 schools involved in the pilot schemes was planning to continue with the project.

An important part of the theory behind the clubs is that they are the children's own territory: a 'neutral' place where they can try out new ways of behaving in the safe presence of reliable and accommodating adults, not connected with their school. Some shy and lonely children will want to try out being noisy and obstreperous, in ways they would never dare 'at school'. Therefore, clubs should have a completely different atmosphere from the children's classroom.

Most schools have been very hospitable to the volunteers, providing extra resources in the form of paper and paint for the children to use, access to sports equipment, and cooking facilities. But it is obviously not easy for schools to have on their territory volunteers running a club, with its own rules and its own ethos. Volunteers have reported occasional difficulties when teachers rushed in to tell children off if they saw them running around or being noisy, rather than leaving the volunteers to deal with things in their own way.

The best solution to occasional tensions between volunteer leaders and teachers is to find somewhere off the site for the club. When this has been possible, it has been very successful. But unless the premises are close to the school, transporting the children to and fro can be time-consuming and awkward for leaders and expensive for the NPT.

One very successful club was held in an adjacent infant school. Another was held in a secondary school that had taken a close interest in the project. Other clubs have used scout huts and community centres.

But the days of cheaply available or free community premises for worthwhile local projects have long since gone. For financial and practical reasons, many clubs will continue to run in the children's school. On balance few schools find this a problem. 'They slip in, do the job and slip out,' said one head teacher.

Heads and teachers had to restrain themselves from intervening in positive ways, such as asking the children to talk about the club at assembly. The clubs are the children's private experience which they might or might not wish to share with the school as a whole. Teachers need to be sensitive to children's feelings on this point.

'I did manage to creep in once, when I had a message for one of the children,' said a head teacher who admitted that he needed great self-control in not asking children about the club, when they were so clearly brimming with enthusiasm about it all. 'They were doing something with a silk sheet and having a fabulous time.'

Response from the Universities

The quality and commitment of the volunteer leaders are essential to the scheme's success. Even with eight hours of training, it is not easy handling eight or ten very disparate children, all of whom, by definition, find social life and relationships difficult.

One tribute to the value of the Pyramid scheme for volunteers is the way colleges and universities have latched on to it as a relevant and worthwhile experience for their students. For many years the West London Institute (now part of Brunel University) provided a steady stream of good volunteers in Hounslow.

When the Pyramid Trust pilot scheme started in Hillingdon, a close link developed with the Psychology Department of the University of Westminster. Several students ran clubs in 1995 and, in the next year, the work became an accredited option for the undergraduate module based on work experience in psychology. Indeed, it is now the most popular option on the course, attracting more than 40 students in 1996.

The students get academic credit for the work, based on a diary they keep of what happens in the club. They also write an extended essay about some particular aspect of the club – perhaps the development of one child, or an analysis of the behaviour of a group of children – relating what happened to their more theoretical studies.

> 'We're very pleased to be able to offer the opportunity to them: they gain so much from the work,' said Dr Paula Hixenbaugh, the head of Psychology at Westminster.
> 'It's also an opportunity to make a contribution to the Pyramid Trust work, which we believe in and admire greatly – I think they're on to something very positive.'

The two universities in Bristol have also supported the scheme. Bristol University has made leading a Pyramid club part of the Special Educational Needs option on its Postgraduate Certificate in Education course, after some of its PGCE students, who had been club-leaders in 1995, had found it to be excellent experience.

At the time of writing, it was too soon for tutors to evaluate how well the Pyramid work helps to meet the needs of students on the Special Needs course. But Dr Terry Atkinson, the director of the Bristol PGCE, had no doubt of the scheme's general value to prospective teachers, and the University will continue to make it possible for all their PGCE students to get involved.

> 'The students get a lot out of it. It allows them to focus on an area that often gets neglected and to work with a particular kind of child in some depth. It's very important for them to learn to understand different types of children and to know more about what happens to children before the age of eleven.'

The University of the West of England has also given invaluable support to the Bristol scheme; students on its primary courses and access courses have become an important source of volunteer club-leaders.

The universities that have become involved with the scheme have made a financial contribution, paying for the training and placements for their students.

Some individual volunteers come into the scheme simply because they hear about it and want to help. They tend to be older, bringing a range of experience and skills to the work. The local Pyramid co-ordinator will take up and check references, carry out a police check and get volunteers to sign statements that they have no criminal record, before allowing them on to the scheme.

Whatever their origins, volunteers all say they find it very satisfying. They enjoy supporting children, giving them a good time and watching how they change over the course of the ten weeks. They seemed almost as sad as the children when the clubs ended.

The Wizzity Club

This is me at the wizzity club. I am praying King ball.

william crew

The best bit was when me mate ice burns and played pass ball.

I have changed by my hair going louder louder. It is a good thing.

Teachers comment.

William was put forward for the club because he was being bullied at school and his confidence needed a boost.
   William is still quite shy in class but there have not been any real problems since.

Figure 22

> *What the children said about the club-leaders*
>
> 'They never shouted at us. They were always nice to us.'
>
> 'Every time I couldn't do something they would help me.'
>
> 'I like them when they tell us what we can do and I like it when we have fun with them and I like it when they were chasing us.'
>
> 'They were my friends.'
>
> 'M. always set all the tables up and gave us shoulder carries home.'
>
> 'I think you are the best baby-sitters.'
>
> 'You look very smart walking with lots of people.'
>
> 'They all cried when we had to go.'
>
> 'Very, very, very nice.'

Multi-professional co-operation

From the beginning, one of the key aims of the Pyramid scheme has been to promote preventive work with vulnerable children by bringing together the different professionals who deal with them: teachers; educational psychologists; child welfare officers; social workers and health workers.

The interdisciplinary meeting at which children are chosen for a Pyramid club and intervention strategies are agreed for many others, is a crucial ingredient in the scheme. Even in schools with excellent arrangements for reviewing the development of all their children, the Pyramid screening and meetings have identified one or two who have 'slipped through the net'.

There will always be some blocks in the way of such multi-professional co-operation. Currently, budget arrangements make it increasingly difficult for educational psychologists to take part. Many local authorities now give schools a financial allocation for educational psychologist time, rather than funding the service centrally. Not surprisingly most schools use the limited money available to try to help cope with children who have the most severe learning or behavioural difficulties.

Another initial difficulty stemmed from the tendency in social and health work practice to rule that children must not be discussed at any meeting unless parents have been offered the chance to be present. In relation to the Pyramid scheme, rigidly applying this rule may lead to the best practice becoming the enemy of the good. No child can take part in a club without written parental consent, but it would greatly increase the demands on the schools if they have to get parents' consent even to mention children at a preliminary meeting.

The Pyramid interdisciplinary meetings have been praised by the professionals involved when they are well planned, when clear information (including the names of the children likely to be discussed) is sent out beforehand to all participants, and when heads and teachers have genuinely welcomed the contributions that outside professionals can make.

A social worker commented that the scheme had great potential in helping all three services, health, social work and education, to fulfil their statutory obligations to children, 'You get three for the price of one,' she said.

'The meeting was the most valuable part of the project from my point of view,' said one head teacher. 'Beforehand we rarely met people from other agencies except in crisis situations. Now links have been forged that will aid communication in the future and thus help all the children.'

CHAPTER 4

The Future

The pilots had a two-fold aim: firstly to test how the Pyramid system could operate most successfully in areas beyond Hounslow, and secondly to develop the procedures and materials that would be needed to make this possible.

By the summer of 1996, when the first two pilots were reaching completion, the scheme had been resoundingly endorsed by its users. All three host authorities were preparing to continue their projects themselves, with funding from a variety of local sources including education, social services and health budgets. In Cardiff, the pilot still had a year to run and was already overlapping with two new unitary authorities; each authority was planning to take over its own scheme.

These successful outcomes reinforced the Trust's ambition for the long term: to spread its method nationally. As the first step towards this end the Trust has adopted a business plan which sets out its strategy for the next three years.

A key principle is that as the Trust's work expands and grows the organisation itself will remain small, with a central office and a core of staff of a director, a national manager and an administrator. A network of regional co-ordinators will be employed to support local Pyramid projects that are owned, funded and managed by their local partnerships.

The Trust's costs will be met in part by its own central fund-raising and in part by fees charged for its work in the regions. A National Lottery Grant awarded in 1996, while not enough to fund the whole development plan, ensured that the Trust would stay afloat for at least three more years.

The NPT Franchise

In return for a contribution to its central costs, the Trust will franchise the Pyramid System to any local project that is able to satisfy two conditions:

- that the necessary administrative framework is provided;
- that the Trust's Performance Criteria are accepted.

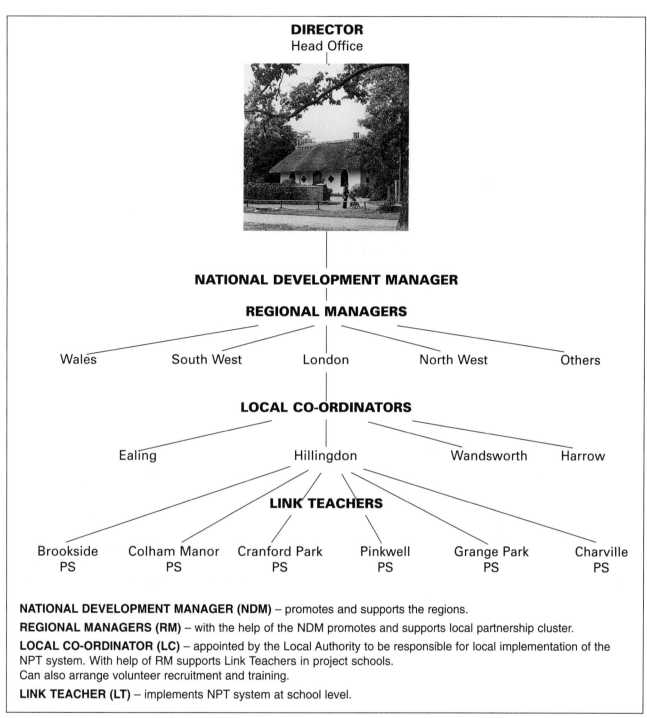

DIRECTOR
Head Office

NATIONAL DEVELOPMENT MANAGER

REGIONAL MANAGERS

Wales   South West   London   North West   Others

LOCAL CO-ORDINATORS

Ealing   Hillingdon   Wandsworth   Harrow

LINK TEACHERS

Brookside PS   Colham Manor PS   Cranford Park PS   Pinkwell PS   Grange Park PS   Charville PS

NATIONAL DEVELOPMENT MANAGER (NDM) – promotes and supports the regions.

REGIONAL MANAGERS (RM) – with the help of the NDM promotes and supports local partnership cluster.

LOCAL CO-ORDINATOR (LC) – appointed by the Local Authority to be responsible for local implementation of the NPT system. With help of RM supports Link Teachers in project schools.
Can also arrange volunteer recruitment and training.

LINK TEACHER (LT) – implements NPT system at school level.

Figure 23 The National Pyramid Trust – proposed structure for development 1996–9

The NPT administrative framework will include:

- a Steering Group or Management Committee with representatives from Education, Social Services, Child Health and from NPT;
- a local Pyramid organiser who recruits schools, involves the support services and arranges clubs and training (typically local organisers will be recruited from the local education service, but a health visitor or community worker could also be suitable);

- a minimum of five participant schools;
- in each school a Pyramid Link Teacher appointed to supervise screening and ID meetings, communicate with club-leaders and provide evaluation and feedback to the Trust. (A national system of accreditation for this role is in the process of validation.)

The Performance Criteria state that the scheme will have succeeded if:

- the designated number of schools participate;
- the designated number of children are screened;
- the needs of children identified as not thriving are assessed by a multi-disciplinary team;
- teachers are advised/supported in their work with each child about whom they have expressed concern;
- a suitable intervention is agreed for each child;
- a suitable number of volunteers to lead the clubs in the designated schools have been recruited;
- the volunteers have been appropriately vetted and trained;
- the designated number of clubs is run;
- the clubs are run to meet the needs of the children, providing love and security, praise and recognition, new experiences, responsibility;
- a review meeting is held at the end to share relevant information and confirm that planned preventative actions have been taken;
- evaluation check-lists have been filled out by teachers before and after clubs.

How the Trust will Support Local Projects

Provided the above structure can be implemented, the Trust will provide the following services, know-how and materials as appropriate for each scheme.

Services:

- The initial training and support for the Local Project Organiser and Link Teacher.
- Support, training and advice to everyone involved in the scheme from members of the Steering Group to support services, school staff and club-leaders. One of the principal tasks of the NPT Regional Co-ordinators will be to develop their expertise in raising funds for new Pyramid projects and to share this with their local partners.
- Recruiting and training volunteer club-leaders, at least in the early stages of a scheme.
- Monitoring and evaluation to ensure that the local scheme is effective.

Materials:

- School Packs – these contain all the information and materials needed for active participation in the scheme, including screening check-lists, meetings records, model letters and many other materials intended to minimise the time needed to operate the scheme at school level.
- Leader Packs – these contain background materials and guidelines on everything from child protection and behaviour management to car insurance and outings, as well as a copy of the Trust's Handbook on all aspects of running a club.

- Local Funding Guide – this was commissioned by the Trust to identify all possible sources of statutory funding for work with children of the kind Pyramid helps. The guide produced 13 possible sources, ranging from Urban Regeneration to Health, Education, Social Services and Volunteering Budgets. The authors discovered a serious gap in information provided by most local authorities about opportunities for funding preventive action which falls into the remit of several different funding departments.

Funding a New Pyramid Scheme

All of the NPT's aims are prominently expressed in the legislation and statutory guidelines that underpin current mainstream policies for children. Thus, the Trust's aims to 'promote child mental health' and 'the welfare of children in need' are as fundamental to Health and Social Services policies as the requirement to meet children's 'special educational needs' is to education policy. Furthermore, there is hardly a policy document concerned with children that does not stress the importance of inter-agency co-operation and prevention.

Most of the sources mentioned in the Trust's Local Funding Guide have already been approached and contribute towards keeping the existing pilot schemes in business. Once the relevance of the work to local authorities' own priorities and statutory responsibilities had become clear, grants have been made from the following budgets: Child Protection, Mental Health Promotion, Truancy and Drug Prevention, Joint Social Services and Health Funding, Special Educational Needs and Volunteering.

Even more significantly, schools themselves have shown that they are prepared to shoulder at least some of the costs of the scheme themselves. Having provided up to £150 towards their club in the scheme's third year, head teachers in one authority have agreed to pay £400 each towards the next round of clubs.

Thus, while it looks very much as though it would be possible to set up a properly funded Pyramid project in any local authority, there will never be one single way of achieving this. The work involved will be much the same in every scheme, although the number of participant schools will affect the total cost. These are two potential funding structures, taken from the opposite ends of the range of possibilities.

Scenario One

- An educational psychologist or EBD (emotional and behavioural difficulties) support teacher already in post is redeployed for 0.2 of his/her time to act as the local Pyramid Organiser, at no extra cost to any service.
- A community or youth worker from Social Services is similarly redeployed for 0.2 of his/her time to carry out the work of recruiting, training and supporting volunteer club-leaders. He/she decides to target mature volunteers from the locality instead of penniless students who need to be paid their – often considerable – travelling expenses. Furthermore, these mature volunteers agree to join a volunteer 'pool' and lead a club every year, thus cutting down on training costs.

- Most Pyramid Link Teachers appointed in participant schools are special needs co-ordinators (SENCOs), who have time allocated for their SENCO work; this eliminates the cost of supplying cover for the Link Teacher's Pyramid work.

In this scenario, the only extra items for which funds will need to be raised are: the direct costs of the clubs, outings and materials and an annual fee to the NPT for supporting the project. All of this could work out at less than £400 per school or £40 per child.

Scenario Two

At the other end of the continuum of possibility is the funding method used in the NPT's pilots. Here an organiser was hired to introduce the Pyramid scheme as an additional service, over and above the authority's standard provision for its children. On top of her salary, all her travel, administrative and management costs had to be found. The volunteers recruited were students who had long journeys to their club locations which had to be paid for. By the third year, when 15 schools were participating, the average cost was £1,200 per school.

It is most unlikely that a management committee, working out a funding structure for a new Pyramid scheme would settle on either of these extreme scenarios. The deciding factors will be determined by local circumstances, but £17,000 would be a reasonable initial target for getting a fifteen-school project off the ground. The on-going costs could well come down to £15,000 p.a.

The following points should be borne in mind:
- Pyramid is a multi-agency partnership; every partner should contribute his/her share.
- Contributions can be in kind rather than money: for example, staff time, transport, providing an administrative base or club premises.
- Even when initially it looks as though the scheme cannot take off because of lack of resources, it will often be possible to fund a scheme by bringing different agencies dealing with children into partnership, and tapping several of the potential sources of money. The Local Funding Guide makes the point that raising funds is hard work and can take two years or more of nurturing even the most promising contact before it bears fruit.

Conclusions

The philosophy of the Pyramid scheme is that:

> 'Every child deserves the chance to have early signs of failure noticed and nipped in the bud. Low cost, positive intervention at an early stage avoids the need for expensive and often ineffective remedial treatment later.'

For several decades there have been increasingly despairing calls for the different services dealing with children, health, education and social services, to work together and to focus on *prevention* as well as crisis services.

Recently, central government has been promoting co-operation more actively. The Department of Health, which has estimated that between 10 and 20 per cent of children will have mental health problems severe enough to require professional help at some stage, has joined in the pressure for more co-operation in the prevention. There is now a statutory requirement for local authorities to draw up Children's Services Plans.

The 1995 government handbook on Child and Adolescent Mental Health, part of the Health of the Nation initiative, also emphasised the need for 'healthy alliances' between all relevant agencies dealing with children and young people.

The only practical place even to consider doing something about early signs of failure is in primary schools. At present such early signs often either go undetected or are not considered serious enough to justify the use of the limited resources for children's special needs.

The Special Needs Code of Practice has not really promoted prevention. The Code's systems were designed for children with evident learning and behaviour difficulties, not for those who, for whatever reason, were failing to thrive socially or emotionally.

The need is for workable frameworks to promote real co-operation between professionals on the ground, based in primary schools and helping significant numbers of children before their problems become deep-rooted and intractable.

The Pyramid scheme offers such a framework, with its well tested, low-cost method to promote successful early intervention.

Furthermore:

- The main intervention strategy is firmly rooted in knowledge about child development.

- The commitment required from schools and busy professionals is limited.
- The energy and cost-effectiveness of volunteers is harnessed, without making daunting long-term demands on their time.
- The work is interesting and challenging. Club-leaders gain considerable satisfaction and reward from seeing the changes in many children's confidence and happiness.
- Help is given to a wide range of children, such as those:
  - whose development has been knocked back by a particular event, such as bereavement or parents splitting up;
  - with a slight or even hidden disability, such as a hearing or speech problem, which makes it hard for them to get along with their peers;
  - who have never learnt the play and social codes that are an essential part of success and happiness at school;
  - with disabled or 'problem' siblings who take up most of the available attention at home;
  - whose home lives, for whatever reasons, are circumscribed and lonely;
  - who have been abused.

For these children the clubs have much to offer, boosting self-confidence, providing a respite from stress and, for those already receiving professional help, adding fun and social confidence to the benefits of more intensive therapies.

Figure 24 An outing can promote confidence

For a short but seemingly critical period, the clubs have shown they can offer all such children the four crucial ingredients picked out by Dr Mia Kellmer Pringle as essential to healthy development: praise and recognition, love and security, new experiences, and responsibility.

The astonishing conclusion suggested by the experience of the Pyramid scheme is that for significant numbers of children, offering these opportunities and meeting these needs just once a week for ten weeks can make a significant long-term difference, allowing them, as one teacher put it, 'to spread their roots and grow strong'.

Appendix A – How four children progressed through the course of their club

J

In July 1996 the Trust received a phone call from a hospital-based occupational therapist asking if someone could come to explain its methods to her department. They had been treating a child for a very long time, but he had made no progress. Recently his speech and motivation had suddenly improved dramatically and the occupational therapist had discovered that this happened while he was at a Pyramid club. The students who ran the club he had attended had realised his needs from the beginning and were able to supply the following notes about his progress.

Profile of J's needs at the beginning of the club

Has recently changed schools and is finding it difficult to make friends. His stammer makes it difficult for him to express himself clearly and fluently. In addition he has experienced many problems at home – and his mother is rather hostile towards the club-leaders.

His progress during the duration of the club

Week 2
Hardly speaking; quite unsure in Circle Time. Doesn't come forward with ideas, sits with S and stammers badly. But there are signs of obvious enjoyment. He feels' special' to be here; not really important *what* he does. Loves praise and mother now very interested in what he does in the club – almost over-concerned about him.

Week 3
Huge improvement. Spoke a lot despite difficulties. Brought in his favourite object and showed great excitement about the trip and the bushy caterpillar (cress). Great enjoyment.

Week 4

Very, very happy today. Smiling and laughing. Last to arrive and still lives in his own world a bit. Danced with his maracca bottle. Had difficulties keeping up with outdoor games. Left until last by the other children in the 'Cat and Mouse' game.

Week 5

Came in very sheepishly because his mum had announced that he had been 'grounded'. Her agitation disrupted the beginning of the club. But J cheered up during the session, delighted by any praise. At first dissatisfied with his mask but with praise became very interested. Showed much greater concentration.

Week 6 – The Trip

Has changed more noticeably than anyone. His stammer seemed to disappear for most of the day until he became tired at the end. He loved the horses and the picnic and participating in all the games. For the first time he was assertive enough to go forward first for the horse ride.

    'I really like horses,' he said.

    'I think they like you too, J,' said P.

    'They must do, mustn't they,' he replied.

    He told his mum that he really enjoyed the day – without a stammer.

Summary

J showed greater improvement than any of the children – possibly because his difficulties were the most pronounced. He started the club nervously, with a significant stammer. He spoke more and more fluently as the weeks went by. Although he stammered when talking about his favourite object, he persisted, expecting everyone to listen and knowing that they would. During the trip he spoke out without fear and with great fluency. His speech therapist has also commented on his improvement.

    With a lot of praise and encouragement, J has developed from being shy, withdrawn and uncommunicative to being more confident and out-going. He has so much more perseverance to achieve. We have affirmed his great personality and sense of humour and he is beginning to see that he deserves to be accepted and liked.

W

Profile at first ID meeting

Described by his teacher as a boy with low ability who rarely smiled and was often tearful. He did not know how to play with other children and in class he was hardly ever on task, disruptive and annoying his class mates. The other children did not want to work with him.

    He is the youngest of two boys; both his brother and mother are suffering from the same chronic disease.

Behaviour in the club

Initially he was difficult to control. His only way of dealing with problems was to be aggressive. He did not understand that difficulties can be overcome through talk or negotiation. He needed to be coerced into taking part in the activities and other club members were reluctant to play with him in activities set up by the leaders because they said he was always fighting. On two occasions W ran off when being taken home.

The club outing seems to have marked a turning point in W's behaviour. After this he appeared significantly calmer and much less disruptive. When he was disciplined after one outburst he vowed never to come to the club again – but he never missed a session.

Profile at second ID meeting

Club-leaders reported that W was more willing to join in the activities and seemed to have realised that by throwing tantrums he does not always get his own way.

His teacher has noticed a dramatic change in his behaviour in class. He is now more frequently on-task although still isolated. In general he seems happier and is less tearful.

When asked about the club, W commented, 'It was good. We had fun and I'm sad they (the club-leaders) left us. They were always nice people. They never shouted at you. I enjoyed the games, the food and the party. I made friends with everyone. It was very nice and very exciting. I liked the outing – I won the bowling!'

S

Profile of S's needs at the first ID meeting

A small, underweight child who appears lethargic and vague. He lacks confidence and doesn't smile or laugh much. Doesn't ask for help in class but simply waits for the teacher. He has been put on SEN register at stage 2. There is a large supportive family.

Progress at second ID meeting

The club-leaders' report
Amazing progress. The most confident child in the club. Has proved to be the club 'entertainer', laughing a lot and liking to make others laugh. Very active – 'Danced if given the chance!'

Teacher's report
He enjoyed the club very much. He has also been getting help with numeracy and literacy for one hour a week after school. His reading is now good.

S's report
I enjoyed playing games like 'spot the difference' and 'had' when it was sunny. I also liked making things – we made a sock puppet. I liked the club-leaders when they told us what we could do and I liked it when we had fun with them and when they were chasing us. K is my new friend – she makes me laugh. But all of them are my friends now. I liked being taken home because we thought what we would do the next week. It was good fun.

A self-assessment questionnaire was carried out with S pre- and post-Club. After the Club S gave eight more positive answers:

He no longer finds it hard to make friends.

Is no longer bothered by the way he looks.
Now thinks he is lucky.
No longer feels left out of things.
Is cheerful.
Thinks he has a pleasant face.
Feels he is easy to get along with.
Thinks he is popular.

K　　　*Profile of K at first ID meeting*

She has difficulty making friends. Comes from a Traveller family and has recently been transferred from another school. Sometimes hides her own things or those of others. Attendance is a problem. Her Mum is very concerned and has difficulty getting K to school as she often complains of feeling unwell.

Progress made by second ID meeting

Report from club-leaders
A bit clingy and dependent on us at first. Now the most boisterous girl in the club and good friends with S. She showed J great kindness when she was upset.

Teacher's report
There has been a lot of improvement in class. She is more confident and has stopped 'losing' things. Seems more relaxed with other children. She now listens and has made a lot of progress socially. She is clearly a lot happier and is showing herself to be more able than at first appeared. Also her Dad is more relaxed with the class teacher.

K's report
I enjoyed it when we made models out of fruit. I made a dog out of a potato and a carrot. The club-leaders were good. I made friends with J and Z and S.

On the self-assessment questionnaire K answered more positively to the eight questions:

No longer feels it is hard to make friends.
Does not think she is unpopular.
No longer feels she is left out of things.
Feels her class-mates think she has good ideas.
Feels she has many friends.
Now thinks she has a pleasant face.
Joins in now instead of watching games.
Feels she is now easy to get along with.

Appendix B – 'It's simple but it works'

A Club-leader's view of the Pyramid Model, by Mark Donati

(Mark delivered this spontaneous report at a NPT reception in Hillingdon Civic Centre, summer 1996.)

I am a psychology undergraduate who came to be involved with the National Pyramid Trust through a work experience opportunity available at my university.

During the club-leader training sessions I came to learn a great deal about the principles that underpin the Pyramid club model. I also became familiar with Schiffer's (1976) theory that the 'club' itself is thought to act as a primary therapeutic agent and that the club-leader's role is merely to 'enable' the group experience.

To me, as a novice club-leader, this theory sounded too good to be true. Placing ten 8-year-old children in a room together and getting them to 'have fun' sounded more like a recipe for chaos rather than an effective way of increasing a child's self-esteem!

But of course, this scenario is a little over-simplified. There are certainly some qualities, like commitment, organisational skills, a sense of fun and enthusiasm and a sense of responsibility that a club-leader needs to have in order to maximise the effectiveness of a Pyramid Club. My co-leaders and I attempted to bring these qualities to each of our club sessions.

By the tenth and final session, we were sure that at least three of the club children had benefited from their experience and this was easily enough to make all our efforts worthwhile.

However, in the week after our last club session, my co-leaders and I attended a Feedback Meeting at the school. Here we were able to hear directly from the teachers about what, if any, positive changes they had witnessed in the club children. However, we were not prepared for what they had to say.

Nine out of the ten children had showed a significant improvement in their self-esteem, self-confidence and general sociability and three of the children had changed completely.

For example, one girl had previously been unable to take constructive criticism of her school work without crying and giving up. Since her participation in the club this girl has overcome her fear of criticism and is now able to respond positively to it. Another girl had been so shy that she barely spoke in class. Since the club she has acted as a messenger for her teacher.

Two other girls and one boy had previously spent a large amount of class time in the First Aid room with the nurse as a way of exchanging the pressures of the classroom for some one-to-one attention. Since the club the nurse hasn't seen them once!

I had hoped to receive some positive feedback but this news was incredible. Within the context of the club, it had sometimes been difficult to see how some of the children had benefited from it. But the pictures painted by the class teachers of some of the children told a somewhat different story. What had we done to bring about such rapid, dramatic and widespread change? It almost seemed to me that some magic must have taken place. It was only at this point that I really understood what Mortimer Schiffer had meant when he talked about the group as being the 'primary therapeutic agent'.

Today, having witnessed at first hand the 'magic' of the Pyramid club model, I believe in it. What's more, I am not alone. I have heard many similar happy stories from other equally amazed club-leaders. But, out of all this what is surely most significant is the fact that such amazing results were achieved with the help of relatively young and inexperienced volunteers. In my opinion, it is this that is the master-stroke of the Pyramid club model, and its implications are tremendous.

The vast majority of children who experience a Pyramid club come out as happier, healthier and more confident young people. Clearly the knock-on effects of this on a social, as well as an individual, level are immeasurable.

When you consider that all this can be achieved easily and cheaply, you wonder why every school, nationwide, doesn't have a Pyramid club! Hopefully one day every school will.

Appendix C – Evaluation by children in two schools

Cherry Lane Junior School

	What did you enjoy most at the Club?	Tell me about the leaders	Did you make any new friends?	Did you like being taken home?	What would you tell other children if they were uncertain about joining the club?
Child A	Playing games – 'Spot the Difference' and 'Had' when it was sunny.	I liked it when they tell us what we can do and I like it when we have fun with them and when they were chasing us.	Yes, K. She makes me laugh.	Yes, because we thought about what we would do the next week. It was good fun.	We played games and they are good club-leaders and they help us make things.
Child B	That we could make things like the things for Mother's Day.	They would help us make things if we got stuck.	J and M.	Yes. Sometimes they would carry our bags. They were nice to us.	It's really fun and you can make a lot of things.
Child C	Making things like masks and cakes. They made a cake when I was off and the leaders brought some of it for me.	They are nice people. They take you to places. We went to London Zoo.	Yes, S. At first he didn't like me. And the leaders.	Yes. I could show Mum everything I made – my brother would eat them.	Don't be afraid – you can make everything.
Child D	We made sock puppets and funny faces. The very first day it was nice when we made our badges.	They were pretty nice.	Everyone that went to the club.	Yes. It was pretty nice to be taken home by someone different for a change. There are people around to talk to.	Join the club, it's fun.
Child E	When we made models out of fruit. I made a dog out of a potato and a carrot.	They were good.	J and Z and S.	It was good.	We made stuff.
Child F	The fun. Making thing like cakes.	They were kind and helpful – I miss them.	Yes, Z and all of them.	I like it instead of my Dad taking me home.	It's OK. It's just an ordinary club; you don't have to be scared. I was happy there.
Child G	Playing games and making things like the sock puppet.	I liked all of them.	Yes, S.	It was nice.	You will like it.
Child H	The party and making sock puppets.	Very, very, very, nice.	They are all my friends.	Yes it was nice when A took me in the car. We took turns.	It's really fun.

Pinkwell Junior School

	What did you enjoy most at the club?	Tell me about the leaders	Did you make any new friends?	Did you like being taken home?	What would you tell other children if they were uncertain about joining the club?
Child A	Cooking.	They were ALRIGHT.	No.	Yes, we went a different way.	You should join because it is good.
Child B	I enjoyed all of it. It was friendly and nice. We can cook and I like that. I liked playing and drawing.	They would help us make things if we got stuck.	All of them.	Yes, we had to walk.	Join because you can play there. We could play what we liked.
Child C	Biscuits and drink.	They are nice and they are kind.	R, M, S and M.	Yes, it was good when we were talking.	It will be nice.
Child D	Games and going outside and the party.	Nice people.	R, D, M and S.	Yes, it was quite good.	*No response.*
Child E	Cooking and playing on the field – 'Hide and Seek' and 'Stuck in the Mud'.	My best one was N. She always took me home.	B, D and S.	Yes, we went by the park and played 'Guess the Word'.	Go because it's good. You can cook there and go on the field.
Child F	Nothing happened.	They were not nice. They didn't listen.	No.	No – I was tired.	Don't go.
Child G	Playing games – the colour game.	They were nice to me.	B, R, M, D, H and B.	Yes – we play 'I-spy' on the way home.	Go if you want to.

References

1 Makins, V. 'Cheap and Cheerful', *Times Educational Supplement*, 10.3.89.
2 Schiffer, M. (1976) 'The Synergy of Children's Groups Psychotherapy and Child Growth and Development', *Group Therapy – An Overview.*
3 Kolvin, I. *et al.* (1981) *Help Starts Here.* London: Tavistock.
4 Kellmer Pringle, M. (1980) *The Needs of Children.* London: Hutchinson.
5 FitzHerbert, K. (1993) *Running a Short-Term Activity Group – A Hand for Volunteer Leaders.* London: The National Pyramid Trust.
6 FitzHerbert, K. (1996) 'Giving Positive Prevention a Chance', *Education* 15.3.85.
7 Skinner, T.C. *et al.* 'Beneficial Effects of Therapeutic Activity Groups for Children at Risk of Maladjustment: Retrospective Evaluation of the National Pyramid Trust Model'. Presented at the British Psychological Society, Development Section Annual Conference, Oxford, 1996.

Further Reading

FitzHerbert, K. (1991) 'The Muppet Club Project – An Alternative Support Service for Children with Emotional and Behavioural Disorders' *TOPIC* (vol. 12, issue 6), Journal of the National Foundation for Educational Research, Slough.
Link, A. (1992) *Mirrors from the Heart – Emotional Identity and Expression Through Drama.* Elora, Ontario: Snailworks Press.
Silveira, W.R. *et al.* (1988) *Children Need Groups.* Aberdeen: Aberdeen University Press.
Tattum, D. and Herbert, G. (eds) (1997) *Bullying in the Home, School and Community.* London: David Fulton Publishers.

If you would like information about setting up a Pyramid scheme, contact:
The National Pyramid Trust
204 Church Road
Hanwell
London W7 3BP
Tel. (0181) 579 5108